Songs of the Marrow Bone

Contributors

Nan Adams
Kellie Campbell
Alan DeLarm
Cheryl Della Pelle
Marc Erdrich
Jane Stinson
Peg Sweeney
Davyne Verstandig
Robley Whitson

SONGS OF THE MARROW BONE

Edited by
Marc Erdrich and Ruth Boerger

HOBO JUNGLE PRESS
Woodbury, Connecticut

Published by Hobo Jungle Press
Woodbury, CT 06798
www.hobojungle.org
©2010 by Hobo Jungle Press

ISBN 978-0-9829945-0-4

Library of Congress Control Number: 2010936574

In Memory of
Jane (Cohen) Stinson
Nan (Nancy Malone) Adams

Contents

Part IV. Grave

Part V. Teneroso

Author Index

Foreword

Fifteen years ago, in 1995, we left our family, home and friends of long-standing to embark on a journey. Feeling guilty and homesick even before we left, we promised we would publish – in due time – the work of a devoted group of writers who, over a period of more than 10 years (and with surprising regularity to this day), met to read and discuss their work.

The years passed and the job was never done; yet the promise, and the guilt, remained. The time to honor that commitment is long past due. Two members of the group have since died, several others have advanced their careers, and all of us have changed in ways too numerous to categorize.

Yet, when it finally came time to begin the task, we realized that over the last 15 years the world has changed dramatically. In 1995, the Internet was only just beginning to show its promise as a means of getting information and ideas to a broad group of people. Today, publishing a book in print as a way of reaching the masses is secondary to publishing on the Internet. Yet for many readers, nothing compares to a book in print.

At first, we struggled with how to go about meeting our original commitment. Should we print the book as promised or should we just publish on the Internet? We argued one way, then the other. Finally, it occurred to us that our angst was unnecessary. We realized we could publish *Songs...* in any medium we wanted, far easier and for less cost than ever before! And we could still be true to the original concept of *Hobo Jungle* by offering new writing to our readers for free.

So, for those of you who prefer the heft of a book we offer this (not for free) paperback version of *Songs of the Marrow Bone;* for those who are accustomed to reading electronically, we direct you to www.hobojungle.org, where you will find all the material included in this book online at no cost. Either way, enjoy.

– Marc Erdrich and Ruth Boerger

Introduction

The writers represented here seem to take a mild sort of perverse pride in having no particular group name or identity. They are the current attendees at what has been, over some ten years of fluid and shifting membership, usually referred to as "workshop." As in "Are you going to workshop tonight? Want a ride?"

Such coherence as they will admit to is largely geographic, centered loosely around Washington Township, Connecticut, although they have attracted attendance, consistent or sporadic, from such surrounding towns as Roxbury, Southbury, Woodbury, Bethlehem, Litchfield, Kent, and as far away as Sharon or Torrington.

In early days, people gathered in what was then the used-book annex of the Hickory Stick Bookshop in Washington Depot, which at that time offered a comfortable sofa and a few chairs for browsers and after hours, occasionally, for writers. In more recent years the workshop has met in a town hall, committee room, in the lobby of a real estate office, and in various people's houses.

The most consistent hosts lately have been Marc Erdrich and Ruth Boerger, of *Hobo Jungle*. It should be noted that Marc has been the instigator, designer, editor, and publisher of this collection. His contribution in both labor and hospitality is beyond measure.

People ask, "But what do you actually do? How do you account for this workshop's longevity?" To answer the first question, we meet twice a month on Wednesday evenings at seven-thirty, and we read to each other. And we listen. And comment, if we feel like it, and ask questions. People who want something to drink, wine or mineral water or whatever, generally bring it with them. Occasionally someone supplies a snack.

As for the longevity question, who knows? Is it the consistent informality and lack of structure? the openness to whatever and whoever turns up? the frequency of the meetings? the insistence on being comfortable rather than business-like?

One thing has seemed to be true of the group no matter who has been attending at any given moment: honest and personal perceptual responses have been preferred to critical rigor. This has meant that everyone has been free to bring rough drafts, experiments, explorations, and undefinable pieces of writing as well as more or less finished work in prose or verse.

For anyone who has ever received interesting answers to the question "Can anyone tell me what I've done here?" no other explanation is needed for why the workshop has lasted, even while individual people have moved away, drifted away, found a group closer to home, or started one of their own. Every single one of them has contributed something, has given something, and, we believe, has gained something.

So the book is dedicated to all the people who have ever come to workshop on a Wednesday night and allowed us to make use of their eyes and ears and voices, their writing, their attention, and their good will.

— *Nan Adams, 1995*

Epigraph

A Prayer for Old Age

God guard me from those thoughts men think
In the mind alone;

He that sings a lasting song
Thinks in a marrow-bone;

From all that makes a wise old man
That can be praised of all;
O what am I that I should not seem
For the song's sake a fool?

I pray – for fashion's word is out
And prayer comes round again –
That I may seem, though I die old,
A foolish, passionate man.

— *William Butler Yeats*

M. Erdrich

Part I
Agitato

Cooking It Up

I've been making stew
all life long, with the marrow of my soul.

And it was like there were specials on personal disasters
in the market this week.

Urgency comes in bunches, but is weighed by the pound.

I was in a wreck, and now
I feel like a wreck, my ankle swollen and tender as if
shoved full of regrets.

My bones and muscles ache so loud, I can barely hear
those fluttering lives around me.

I knew my brakes were not up to being emergency brakes,
but assumed I could avoid emergencies.

So why do I ignore warnings?

I watched myself be out of control. Terror happened,
even before the bang and yells.

It just so happened my car was packed with my history. In
the collision, photographs and messages stormed furiously
over me. My loved ones faced me. Photos of myself, too,
stared up at me (some taken in the darkness of my worst
moods, in the loneliness of disbelief, when I didn't trust my
lover, myself, or my world).

It hit me: a person's past sweeps by as he drowns…
Was I drowning? Naah, but…
I was in a serious situation, and absorbed the bleakness for
     a long time….

3

This pull between OK or not.

When I got back to my tiny cottage, I continued making
    the stew.

Reluctantly put new sorrow in.

It matters what goes in this.
I know it does.

Too much bitterness is easily caused. A heavy hand
    anywhere is disastrous.

All this emergency feeling now, so
there's a wacky balance to the stew.
It's a pity: there's too much self-pity.
I've got a lot of angst to use up; about as much as I can
    stand.

A badly bruised conscience, too.
I throw that in.

Now what?

I have to remain the cook. I can't let the ingredients take
    control.
 The stew's had a lot of luck already. And wonder. And the
    great nuances of love.

But I admit it needs more of something; something new.
Everything is as tenuous as understanding.
The phone rings. It's a concerned friend, worrying about me.
"I hear you're in a crisis," he says. I grab a dictionary, to
read the definition: "that point in a disease when a
decisive change occurs, leading to either health or death".
I gulp, and say, "I'm working on this stew, is all. It keeps me
going. I threw in a cosmic day full of demons, but tomorrow

I hope to add a cosmic day full of angels.
Real deliciousness comes when it balances out."

There's no recipe for this. It's all intuition.

— Alan DeLarm

May 1936, with Aunt Margaret

Its frequent floats between Frankfurt and Lakehurst, New Jersey, had captivated Miss Margaret Mather's lucid blue eyes. She had admired the huge silver shape of the 800 foot Zeppelin, entranced by the stillness in its smooth motion.

Through a cool mist the passengers were escorted towards the airfield by stoic German soldiers who inspected every stocking and toothpaste tube with unusual suspicion.

The dirigible was tethered and rocking restlessly beside its mammoth hanger. Spectators and Nazi boys were waving as Miss Margaret crossed the narrow gangway onto the airship's passenger deck.

From ceiling to floor pearl-gray linen dressed the interior. Long sloping windows tilted open, she could hear a brass band below. The captain called "up ship". Mooring ropes were loosened and with a quick lift, then pull, upwards the Hindenburg joined the clouds, drifting over vast beech woods and twinkling villages. Hilltop beacons guided them along rapidly out to sea.

Aunt Margaret dined at the captain's table. They shared a lust for adventure. He said that the strong storms that surrounded them would do nothing more than cause dramatic white caps below.

Glistening icebergs and full spectrum rainbows encircled Newfoundland. The airship was saluted by Boston harbor water vessels and small airplanes buzzed for a clear glimpse. Some followed along. Bursting yellow forsythia splashed against green hay fields spotted with apple trees in full spring bloom. Dogs barked madly. Deer galloped into pine forests for shelter. Cars pulled over and tooted their horns.

Tall buildings were enveloped into the New York skyline by thick grey clouds. Passengers wept as they cruised the Bronx, then Harlem, down Fifth Avenue, past bridges, and out towards New Jersey. Home was spectacular in Miss Margaret's view.

Thunder rolled over the Hindenburg and flashes of lightning filled the sky. The first landing was aborted. Aunt Margaret didn't care how long they circled. She wrote in her journal, changed her dress, then joined the other passengers on deck.

A jolt.

Then the mooring ropes were tossed out. The landing crew rushed forward to draw the great silver dirigible down. A dull muffled pop came from the engines, the ship lurched forward and she was hurled against the far end wall. Other bodies pinned her. Aunt Margaret couldn't breath. She stayed down, others jumped up until blue and red flames shot in like a tongue. People screamed. Impaled against the metal trimmings, charcoaled, streaming with blood, some shot out the windows, many died instantly. The lapels of her coat let her hide and still see horror.

"Hey Madame, come out." She couldn't realize what was left of the ship burnt on the ground. A limo became an ambulance, a shop became the hospital. She didn't know how many people were there because there were too few to count. Aunt Margaret's hands were blackened and burnt flesh was the air. A semi-conscious steward raised his head and with full respect said "Miss Margaret Mather, your coat's melted to your body! And do you know that you're missing a shoe?" She didn't.

— *Kellie Campbell*

Crazy Man

Crazy man in a crazy town
striding down the sidewalk
talking to someone:
urgent, urgent —-
talking into a red telephone
with the cord trailing behind
plugged into nowhere,
red phone hot-line:
urgent, urgent —
veering over to some curbside cans
and pulling off the clatter lids.
Five cans full of great stuff!
  Call you back...
  All right...
  Keep you on hold...
  Gotta talk to the garbage now.
Urgent, urgent.

— Robley Whitson

Coming and Going
among the Trees

November wind tunnels down the fire-trail,
underfoot, horse droppings mush into mud,
a shot-gun blasts the nearby wood
as I worry the good of my red coat.

Keep walking. I spit out mantra words
that pierce through chill air,
some syllables fall onto shit,
heel them, grind them in good
know here they will grow fast.

Stray seeds of prayers and faint hopes
all beg for the ground,
all mingle blood and water.
I keep walking straight as the pines
who brush a cheek, grab a pull of hair

and speak so slowly,
sometimes it takes all day to hear one word.

They rush out green. I run a breath out.
"Find the cost of freedom, buried in the ground.
Mother Earth will swallow you, lay your body
down."

Song. Sung. Signs in the wilderness
point to a life of saplings bent,
stripped of tender bark from deer rubs.
God help us, those itchy antlers.
For a woman who keeps walking,
a rapid heartbeat is only the beginning.

— *Cheryl Della Pelle*

Meanwhile, between Crises

it is necessary to observe
that the sky has been a particular shade of blue
for two days now; and that the Labrador
stinks characteristically of pond water;
and that the sun, ah, yes, the sun, minding
its own business, misses this leaf and
hits that one; and the mind of my elder daughter,
in its quaint intellectual corsets, cheers me as much
as the rest of her (uncorseted);

and pushing, once, up from the grimy sleet
of a Long Island airport, the Whisperjet
broke through the winter ceiling and came out
above it where the sun, minding its own business
as usual, was making alpine landscapes
on the roof in every blinding shade
of white except for white;

and that (although
I myself prefer exuberance)
there is something to be said, perhaps,
for the strict aesthetics of a power failure.

– Nan Adams

To Shoot a Coyote

You wake me with a twisted howl,
not the clear hawoo that rises cleanly,

A choke of torment catches my throat,
eyes strain the dark room for a reason.

— Cheryl Della Pelle

Women's History

I

Women, hidden away
for eons of time,
lost or found
in their aprons and wash.
Clinging to images
handed down by
worn and tired mothers
harping on how to be
who to be –
seeking men to answer
their needs.
Centering their lives
on a man's time clock.

II

Women now, dressed
in finer clothes
labeled with magic names,
cling to images of Independence
handed down by mothers
thinking Independence was freedom
only to look into eyes
of latch-key children
dulled by television's noise.
Women centered now,
from nine to five.

III

The biological clock
ticks on and on.
Relentlessly greying hair,
weakening bones, dulling muscles
ovaries and wombs unused,

or used too late become
life threatening.
Breasts are smoothed by creams
unsuckled by young mouths.

Whose image to follow?
Whose eyes will reflect our own?
What is quality time?
Wherein lies our center?

— *Peg Sweeney*

HIV Positive

Because she risked a midnight indiscretion,
she could shake the cold hand of death.
As the airplane moved her towards Colorado,
her veins could contain a vicious, horrifying plague.

She could shake the cold hand of death,
with her body in torture and her mind frozen.
Her veins could contain a vicious, horrifying plague,
and ignorant people would point and stare.

With her body in torture and her mind frozen,
she could be stripped of precious dignity.
And ignorant people would point and stare,
while the government holds back funds for research.

She could be stripped of precious dignity,
make friends in treatment who would also die.
While the government holds back funds for research,
she must find options and hang onto threads.

Make friends in treatment who would also die,
because she risked a midnight indiscretion,
she must find options and hang onto threads,
as the airplane moved her towards Colorado.

— *Kellie Campbell*

Part II
Appassionato

The Witch Tree

Part 1. Joe

Only a Christian, a Bible-Swinging, Hallelujah-Singing, Fall-On-Your-Knees-and-Beg-Forgiveness Christian would have named them Baptism Falls. The Ojibway had named them Tettegouche which meant "falling water", or maybe it was "high water". Joe had forgotten most of the Ojibway language he ever knew. He moved lightly through the life burgeoning everywhere beneath his feet, hoping to avoid crushing any part of it, imagining the lushness of the greenery that would fill this place by late June. Patches of snow decorated shadowy places, untouched by the early spring sun, awaiting the shifting of the planet to a more advantageous position. The tiniest of white flowers promised to open fully by late-afternoon but Joe could not wait.

The high path up to the falls was still laced with almost-melted iciness so he took the lower path that climbed gradually up the back of the cliff. The footing was surer, even though walking it meant fighting the sharp tearing branches of the heavy underbrush. Taking a fall here could be calamitous. He did not intend to fall and break part of his body so that he might be trapped here to starve to death or be discovered by a pack of wolves that would tear him apart, piece by piece.

He might consider jumping from the height of the falls when he got there. They were high enough to guarantee a swift fall to death. He wouldn't even have to jump. He could just stand near the edge on a rock and slip accidentally into the relentless rush of the water to be swept over the edge of the cliffs, and then be caught up in the final scheme of things.

He pushed his way through the thick brush that survived under the protection of the tall pines, breaking a thousand tiny, still-frozen branches as he moved, wondering what a plant felt in winter, wondering what he felt in winter, whether his mind froze around

19

the edges when the ground froze, or whether his emotions congealed from November through April, so that he was unable to deal rationally with reality.

He knew this path he was following up the back side of the falls, and the high, steep one, as well as he knew the stairs in his and Becky's house, rough-hewn, unsanded lumber cut from the trees of the reservation, as unfinished as their lives and their work. From their studios on the second floor they looked out on Lake Superior, the huge inland fresh water sea that maintained a vision of perfection for the mind. The acreage above the lake where he and Becky had built their house was a piece of land Joe had loved from the time he was a kid.

Dad had often taken him there just to sit and study the lake and sky and how they blended into each other, blues stretching to the empty horizon, and then again blues rising vertically to the beginning of time and space. It was the only place for their house so Joe had asked the Tribal Council for that land. It would make an inviolable aerie where he and Becky would dwell with all the spirits of the lake and sky and there paint magnificent pictures for them.

Joe pulled himself up over the top of the cliff and stood in icy aloneness alongside the river as it plunged down the water-smoothed stone and ran wildly away towards the lake, churning and flashing against the iron red rocks of the river bed, a fantasy of sunlight and water that sparkled brilliantly in his eyes and made them tear. He stepped tentatively onto a wet rock. It would be simple if he just slipped. But he didn't slip. Perhaps it wouldn't work anyway. Perhaps it would only be an accident. Broken legs or hips or backs were not on the agenda. He might use the small revolver he carried for protection to end abruptly all thoughts, all hatreds, all disappointments and all possibilities. This was his land, the land of his grandfathers, an eternity removed from the white civilization of the city where he had to go to sell his art.

He did sell his art. His last canvas had sold for almost $200,000. He was doing well. They were doing well. Their house, the one he had dreamed, before he commissioned an architect had been in the most prestigious architecture and home magazines. "A triumph of design and function," one writer called it when first designed. Tourists had come in such numbers to see it and hopefully meet the great man that Joe finally put up No Trespassing signs to keep them away and a gate to ensure they didn't ignore the signs.

Becky didn't like the gate or the signs. She liked company because it distracted her from her painting. Visitors kept her from recognizing that her work was not going well. Joe took her things with him to the Twin Cities and tried to get his agent interested but he wasn't. Sometimes in the summer when tourists streamed through the area Becky would sell her paintings to tourists who were looking for souvenirs of their trip. She got $100 for one portrait of an old woman doing bead work. So far that was the monetary zenith of her work.

From the top of the cliff Joe could see the lake. It was calm and still. From here there was no hint of the ugliness of Duluth and Two Harbors or Silver Bay where the ores wrenched out of the earth up on the Mesabi were loaded into the boats that would sail the Great Lakes, through the Soo Canals down into Erie and the great steel mills of Pittsburgh.

Here, on the height of Tettegouche the lake was what it was, a tear drop from the Great Spirit. One might even try walking across it today, a glistening sapphire and then just slip away into its great icy depths to be at one with it. But it was too cold to pursue any thought more than briefly.

Joe slid part of the way down the hill and picked up the lower path back to the parking area and his car. He was thoroughly frozen. He turned on the car heater full blast, and then poured a cup of coffee from his thermos to warm his throat and thaw his body.

He had learned over the years of driving up from Minneapolis and his agent and the openings and cocktail parties to carry hot coffee in a quart thermos. The house was another hour ahead.

21

Perhaps she would be there, waiting for him, glowing with success at the easel. Perhaps her eyes would be shining again, the way they used to, the way they had when he first met her ten years ago.

From the first moment he saw her in his painting class at the college, dressed in jeans and a long white linen shirt he had adored her. She wasn't the first white student who had attracted him nor the first with whom he had an affair. But Becky was the first white woman he had loved. He found himself lecturing directly to her, quite unable to take his eyes from hers in the classroom.

She had been a delight to the eye. Her figure was perfectly proportioned. Her mouth was exactly the right width, her eyes widely-spaced, her cheek bones almost as high as his own. But he wasn't attracted to her because of that physical perfection or because her skin was the color of the palest pink rose, her hair so long and so soft he wanted to own it. Her long thighs and perfectly rounded breasts were cheap commodities in his life as an artist.

What had caught his breath was how her whole body moved in rhythm with earth rhythms. Her consciousness was so elevated that she spoke to him without speaking. Their love was perfectly fulfilled, physically and emotionally despite an age difference. He was thirty-five and she a bare nineteen.

The difference only enhanced his sense of needing to protect her and her feeling of security in him. His passion for her had once ignited joy and delight. Now it filled him with thoughts of death.

They lived in Minneapolis for a time but once she saw the north shore of Lake Superior she was never happy in the city again. Perhaps that had been his first mistake. He should not have shown her the reservation.

As they drove north from Duluth along the shore on that first trip home, Becky was intoxicated by the colors of the water, the forests, and the cliffs with their plunging waterfalls. She fell in love with the beauty and made Joe fall in love with it again.

She nagged and begged and pleaded until they left the city. It was hard to give up the teaching and the feeling of belonging to academia he had enjoyed, but it had given him time to paint as he had never painted before. He sometimes spent ten hours a day painting, as if there were not enough time to finish his projects.

At first Becky had been completely happy. In some strange sense she had come home. She learned all of the legends and history of his people. She became Ojibway.

At first she would spend an afternoon or two during the week at the gift shop in the center of the village, talking to the tourists, telling them the history of the handicrafts for sale or perhaps one of the legends of the Ojibway. If they were interested she might even drive them out to see the Witch Tree.

From the first time she saw it Becky was entranced by that incredible tree that hung out high above the lake, its trunk torturously twisted by the winds that swept around it endless season after endless season, century after century, even before the first European explorers discovered it.

The fascination was not just with the twisting of the Tree but with the illusion that it had no root system in the earth that embraced it. There was a root. If one explored the circumference of the Tree one could find a slender root that anchored it in the ground and supplied the nutrients required for life.

But Becky chose to ignore that almost invisible root and spoke only about the Tree as being without roots, making it a tree of remarkable magic. The Ojibway regarded it that way and Becky outdid the Ojibway on the subject. She began to go there at least once a week, always taking some tobacco along to leave at the base of the Tree as her gift to the spirit of the Tree. She tried desperately to paint the Tree, as though if she could capture the ethereal disconnectedness of it she could somehow explain her own existence.

Early in the morning she packed the Jeep with her sketch pad, canvas and easel, her paints, brushes, pencils, charcoals, and pens, and drove the ten miles up to the dirt road to the Tree. It wasn't an easy drive but only unreasonable weather kept her from her obsession. Her studio was filled with sketches and paintings of the Tree. None of them were good so they weren't hung. They stood in stacks against the wall, reproaching her for her inadequacy.

Joe had suggested she take a couple of courses at the university in Duluth but she didn't want to leave the reservation. It had become her home, with the built-in safety net, the people who accepted her for what she was. The women in town liked her because she was sweet and kind and helpful and loved the handicrafts they made and tried to sell. The old men loved her because she pried old stories from them and was ever eager to learn more about the old ways. The young men liked her because she was pretty and fun.

They loved Becky the way they had never loved Joe. Joe didn't quite belong to the reservation any more. Perhaps he never had. Perhaps he had always been just an observer and not a participant. From the time he was old enough to go to school he had wanted to get away from the reservation and its poverty and hopelessness. He didn't want to leave his family but there was no way to make money on the reservation.

He made too much money now. His house was four times the size of anyone else's. He drove an expensive all-terrain vehicle to manage the back roads of the reservation.

He put the other men on the reservation to shame and they hated him for shaming them. He was their success story, proof that even an Indian could succeed in the white world and they hated him for that.

Joe passed the new motel on the right side of the road, overlooking the lake. It was big and tastelessly conceived but it would undoubtedly do very well because it was the last accommodation before the reservation. Tourists rarely stayed on the reservation. They only came to look from a safe distance.

In his mind he could imagine Becky standing at the easel, finally making an artistic breakthrough, past the terror of her childhood with the alcoholic mother and incestuous stepfather. She had to get past that point or her painting would remain what it was when he first met her – schoolbook work with a certain charm but without insight or imagination. Sometimes Becky cried at night in bed when they were through making love because the love-making would be forever fruitless. Becky had been permanently damaged by her brutal step-father and there could be no children. But that was just as well. Becky herself was a child. There had been three psychiatrists, three modes of therapy, three failures. Becky did function, but not as an artist and that was all she had come to want.

Perhaps today had been different for her. Perhaps today she forced herself past the ugliness and into the child she had been once long ago.

Joe drove down the long driveway toward their house, forcing a smile. He promised himself he would not ask her how her painting had gone while he was away. She always said when he had to go to Minneapolis that she would stay behind and work, that this time, being alone, with no distractions, she could make the breakthrough that meant her happiness. So Joe always asked how it had gone when he arrived.

But this time he would not. He would just talk about the drive back and where he stopped for lunch. No mention of stopping at the falls.

The stereo was playing full blast when he went in the house but he didn't see Becky. She had loaded some New Age junk into the CD player. They had an extensive library of good CD's that she could play but she never did. He shut off the stereo and wandered through the house. She didn't answer when he called to her. Becky was nowhere. The living room was a mess. Empty beer cans, half-empty plates, and overfull ashtrays cluttered every table top. He climbed the stairs to the bridge that spanned the living room and connected their studios with the bedrooms.

Their own bedroom was deserted, the bed unmade, large piles of her clothes draped over the chaise and the black lacquer ladderback chair he had bought for her in St. Paul. He knocked on her bathroom door. There was no answer. He pushed open the door and then recoiled at the musty smells of wet towels and un-scrubbed tiles. The mirror over the sink reflected the total disarray of the room and of Becky's life. Joe gathered the towels and shoved them into the hamper.

He went into the hall and listened for any sound. The silence was complete. He knew she wasn't in her studio. From the bridge he looked down on the living room he had conceived with such joy, conceived with a picture of Becky always in his mind. He had decorated it with unthinking extravagance to please her but it had been a useless extravagance that had brought them no joy.

Becky was not in the house. She was not in her studio. He knew that but he had to see for himself. There was no sign that she had been in the room while he was away. Her brushes were dry and un-cleaned. A half-finished portrait of a woman stood on the easel. It was like a half-dozen such portraits she had painted of her friends and neighbors, but the woman in every one of the portraits had the empty eyes and tight, thin mouth of Becky's mother. He went down into his studio where his new canvas awaited him. He had mounted it on the wall because of its ten foot by fourteen foot size. The painting he planned would depict the Battle of New Ulm, one of the highlights of the great Sioux uprising in Minnesota in the 1860s. He had researched the battle with the greatest care, as he had researched each of his historic paintings. No one could quarrel with his scholarship.

They sold well to white insurance companies and banks whose large walls demanded large canvases. Their presence seemed to assuage the consciences of corporate officers because they were supporting an Indian in his work. The officers of the insurance companies and banks told him that women often became teary-eyed when they viewed the scenes he painted, overcome by the portrayal of atrocities committed by their ancestors against the Indian people. Joe listened to the stories. He was sure that the ladies recovered quickly and were able to complete their financial arrangements without further interference from their souls. White businessmen were his clients and he was their property. He belonged more to them than he did to his own people. At least Becky tried to paint the reality of the reservation. He hadn't tried since he was a very young man and awed by his own talent for drawing.

Becky would be back soon, probably. She knew he was coming home today. Maybe she had started something for dinner.

He wandered into the kitchen and looked in the refrigerator for a beer. None there. It had been drunk by a lot of freeloaders who never hesitated to take advantage of Becky. He slammed the door shut so hard that the refrigerator vibrated for a moment with the violence.

She was probably down at the cafe swilling mugs of coffee with her friends. In the last few months she had taken to spending a lot of time at the cafe. There was always somebody there, usually lots of somebodies who would love to hear her funny stories. She used to tell funny stories about Joe – "the professor" she liked to call him – in a loving way. When she told them lately it was to make fun of him.

"Big Brave Professor," she called him now. "Heap Big Brave Chief Professor. Big Money. Big Shot." The creeps who hung out at the cafe would love her derision of him, Joe knew. He finished his beer and made himself some coffee. They would follow up her funny stories with imitations of Joe, how he walked and talked. Becky was the Indian and he was the outsider.

He was 48 now. Becky 32. The age difference hadn't mattered at first. It mattered now because Joe was reaching the end of his life and Becky's was just beginning. His father had died at 45. His mother at 29. His one brother out in California had died last year at 51.

There wasn't much time left. It was a question of waiting for it to happen to him or making it happen himself, thereby insisting to the end that he had some control over his life.

He wandered back to his studio and looked at the Battle of New Ulm. In the good white history books it was called the Massacre of New Ulm because the Sioux had won. Tonight it didn't seem to matter whether the painting was ever finished or not, whether the colors were right, or the bodies right or the horses right or the sky and ground right. Nothing seemed to matter tonight.

Perhaps Becky was not at the cafe. Perhaps she was at the Witch Tree trying to determine how she could connect with the reality of life again. He looked out at the Great Lake that lay beyond him. In the darkness it was an indiscernible entity. The moon was disappearing behind clouds that looked heavy with snow. He put a new canvas up on the easel and prepared to work. There was a picture in his mind that had nothing to do with battles, dying soldiers or warriors or horses.

He reached for a brush and blended the paints into a pale gray color tinged with blue. He worked the color onto the canvas, unaware of what he was painting until the first strokes defined the trunk of the Witch Tree. He watched with fascination as he painted, his unplanned, unbidden ideas growing on the canvas, undirected by him, directed by the grandfathers who lived in him, unknown until tonight, rejected until tonight. They had always known the Tree and now Joe knew it in his hands and his soul.

Becky would know when she saw it. She would understand immediately what had happened, that he had finally come full circle and was in full harmony with his own past. It would save Becky and explain to her her own disconnectedness. The blues blended into blues, the gray-white fragility of the Tree interspersing the power of the sky, of the lake, of the land. Each stroke was surer, stronger, more definite as he pursued his vision until, finally, the effort of capturing that vision made his hand tremble and blurred his eyesight.

He forced himself to stop. Becky would be home any minute now. Joe needed to clear his head before she got there. She would know that he was working in the studio when she arrived because it was the only room in the house in which there were lights. She would come looking for him and find the painting. She would come looking for him and find herself. He would give her five or ten minutes by herself to consider what it all meant.

He went outside and climbed down the outside steps that led to their patio overlooking the lake. The lake was almost still in the mist of the evening. The red and gray boulders that lined the shore below him were lightly covered by snow that now fell softly on his head.

Above him, in the house, lights went on, first in the front hall, then in the living room, then over the stairs and across the bridge. Joe smiled to himself. Becky was home. She always came home, finally.

Part 2. Becky

The ancient Tree was tormented beyond reason, twisted and pulled into a grotesque parody of a tree, a statement of life to be pondered again and again, one ponder to match each ring. Of course no one knew how many rings there were inside the Tree. Only cutting it down would provide the answer. She did know that the first French explorers in the region had made note of the Tree hundreds of years before.

Becky positioned her body on a reasonably flat rock on the north side of the Tree. She opened her sketch pad and tried again to capture the nature of its disconnectedness. How many times had she tried? She had lost count. It wasn't a big tree. Its bark was abused and thin. It had few branches and they were but fragile imitations of themselves. It hung out on a high bluff above Lake Superior, unprotected from the iced winds that screeched straight down from the Arctic Circle much of the year.

There was a root. If you looked behind the Tree down on your hands and knees you could see it, a single, slender root that had worked its way down past the rocks into the warm earth, searching out a home, finally anchoring itself tenuously in the rich soil. The lake lay beyond and below the Tree, a great ocean of water deep blue under the late winter sky, the perfect backdrop for the Tree the Ojibway called the Witch Tree. They were quite correct. It was pure magic, not just its precarious, unexplained existence, but something in its nature that was magic, that spoke to Becky, and drew her back to it again and again.

Joe was tolerant of her obsession with the Tree. He could have been unpleasant about it and called her a fool, even forbade her trekking off by herself in the wilderness. She knew she should let Joe come with her once in a while to reassure him that he was a part of her life with the Tree. But it would have been a lie. He was not part of it. He was part of the real world where he was a success with his paintings. Before that he had been a success as a teacher at the university. Before that he had been on his way to success, marked from the beginning by his talent and ambition. The Witch Tree belonged to Becky. It was the one thing in her life that was hers alone. Joe's smothering love had no place here in the high, rough grasses of the bluff where only an occasional gull dropped by out of curiosity.

Becky sketched quickly with her charcoal, her eyes almost closed. She had no need to see the Tree with her eyes. That was the problem. It was her soul that hadn't quite yet seen the Tree and until it did she would not understand it or herself. She pulled the paper off her pad and crumpled it up, stuffing it in her big tote so as not to litter her sacred place. She opened a cigarette and spilled its contents of shredded brown tobacco around the base of the Tree in solemn remembrance of its sacred nature, repeating the words taught to her by the old women in town.

Joe would be back tonight. She had promised him a fish and wild rice dinner but she knew she wouldn't bother with it. There was enough laundry to keep her busy for days but she wouldn't go near it. She had promised to clean the house and she hadn't done that either because she didn't care whether the house was clean or not. It was too big to begin with. The cathedral ceilings were unreachable except by ladder. The wide wooden floorboards were eternally dusty. The huge glass walls facing the lake were always dirty, even twenty-four hours after she cleaned them. The house overwhelmed her with its demands, just as Joe overwhelmed her with his demands to own her and return his passion. She had dreamt a half-dozen times now of lightning striking the house and setting it ablaze in a magnificent bonfire.

Once she had loved him. Once he had been bright with enthusiasm for teaching and ideas but he didn't seem to care any more. He only cared about making money and about her. His adoration which had once protected and cushioned her now enveloped and suffocated her. It required her to be kind to him and not shatter his adoration which was inextricably tied up with his own identity. She was responsible for his joy or lack of joy every minute of every day and night. She was learning to hate him for it.

A single white gull soaring over her head called raucously into the wind. Becky couldn't imagine that it was marking its territory in the sky. There was plenty of room for thousands of gulls in the sky above her. It was only when the gulls landed on the shores of the lake that they fought over space.

She packed up her sketching equipment and headed back for town. She put the Jeep in low gear and roared up out of the small dusty pocket where she had parked and onto the dirt road leading to the main highway and town. A tall cloud of dust swirled up behind her as she lurched down the road. She and the Jeep belonged to each other on this road where the ruts and rocks were part of the reality. The Jeep had been Joe's present to her last Christmas and for a moment she had loved him for it.

The jolting motion of the ride disappeared on the black pavement of the state highway with its neat yellow and white lines. She didn't want to go home and wait for Joe. By four o'clock she would be in a panic because she had done no painting since he left three days ago. By five she would be in front of her easel slashing at the canvas in the fury that accompanied her work now. By six she would begin to fix the fish and rice dinner she had promised him. By seven she would have spent herself. By eight Joe would be home.

The counter at George's cafe was full at three. It was full most of the time. George's was about the last place left on the reservation where Becky still felt as though she belonged. It was mostly a male hangout and the males at George's appreciated Becky. They just liked the chance to enjoy her lithe body and pretty face, whether through wide-open, half-closed, and even through closed eyes when they could imagine what she looked like without her jeans and sweater.

Becky hopped up onto a stool next to ever-present Tommy and punched him playfully on the arm. He was a good-looking kid, probably not more than 20 or 21, and unemployed, like most of the men on the reservation. He was tall, well-built, and not stupid. She wondered if he had ever tried a different cafe or the bar over at the big motel, maybe gone up to Thunder Bay just for the hell of it or down to Duluth for a big weekend on the town.

"How's it goin'?" she asked Tommy and then slapped the counter with the flat of her hand. "Right here!" she demanded of old George. He obligingly put a mug of hot coffee in front of her.

"Hey, Babe," Tommy said, returning her little punch. He looked her up and down and up again with the utmost appreciation. "You know," he observed casually, switching his attention from her to himself by staring straight ahead into the mirror behind the counter, "you got the best ass in town – maybe the whole reservation."

"Yeah, and it belongs to Joe," she replied.

"Someday when he's out of town gettin' rich you'll be ripe. You can call me then. Ain't nobody better'n me, girl." He adjusted his hair to a more flattering configuration.

"Joe's better'n you," she replied. She waved to Peggy Gordon at the other end of the counter.

Peggy was a nice kid. She thought Joe was terrific. She was one of the few people around who thought so.

It hadn't been like that when they first came back to the reservation. Joe had been gone for many years and was only an occasional visitor. He was the guy who made it big down in the Twin Cities. But when they came back here to live and built the house out on the lake everything changed.

Even the old ladies down at the fort who made bead necklaces and bracelets for the tourists and who had loved Becky at first, began to hear the stories about Joe's house and the twelve-foot leather couch in the living room and the painting studios that were big enough to house whole families. Becky invited people to visit and they did but that only made it worse so she took to hanging out in town for company. With every passing year they were more imprisoned in the beautiful big house on the lake.

You got it made," Peggy had said to Becky one evening when they were sitting at a table in the bar by themselves. The Vikings were playing the Bears in a Monday night game so the girls were left alone. "Joe's rich, ain't he?"

"Yeah, pretty," Becky agreed.

"You got that cool house," she sighed. "I'd do anything for a house like that. How about letting me come and take care of it for you? I'll just find a nice corner where I can sleep. You can paint all day. I'll clean and cook and you won't have to do nothin'."

"Yeah, you'll clean and cook and steal Joe," Becky said. They laughed.

Peggy said it again now as she slid her rounded body onto a stool next to Becky. She shook her long black hair away from her face and fixed Becky with her dark brown eyes. "Let me clean your house," she pleaded. "I need work real bad. Mom's arthritis is real bad. I got to get her medicine for it."

Becky was silent. She looked away from the intense eyes. "I could shine the floors for you," Peggy said. "Do all the laundry, ironing, even some cooking if you wanted."

Becky considered. Joe probably wouldn't mind the hundred or so a week it would most likely cost. He'd probably think it would be good for Becky to be freed up to work on her own painting. She let her mind float along the path of freedom for a moment, imagining working at the Tree for a whole day unfettered by dirty floors or laundry or cooking. She could see herself in front of her easel, finally freed to be the artist she was meant to be, absorbed in her creation.

She would also be free, she realized suddenly, for Joe's passion. The thought worked through her mind. She would be available without excuses to be led at any time to their bed for another bout of sex and another prolonged declaration of love. Her reverie ended as Tommy leaned into her face and seductively moved his hand across her back.

"Let's move the party to your place, Beck," he said. "I got two six-packs in the car. I'll grab them and we'll go party at your place, Beck."

"Come on, Becky," Peggy urged. "You can show me the house and tell me just the way you want me to do things."

Becky could never refuse them. They were fun and this afternoon she needed fun. It was almost 5:30. Joe would be home by 8 or 9. He would probably stop for a break. If he had left Minneapolis at two as he said he would he'd need a break when he got to Duluth. He'd stop for a cup of coffee or a drink at the hotel there he liked so much. She could get them out of the house by 7:30.

Becky put her foot down hard on the accelerator. The tires of the Jeep squealed a high complaint as she cut through the parking area and onto the highway. Ten years ago she would have been intoxicated with the camaraderie of the group, knowing that she belonged with these people as she had never belonged to her own family. Ten years ago she gloried in being a part of the Indians who existed here in the northern forest apart from the main thrust of civilization. She had loved the faces and the stories, the myths and legends of the lake and forest.

Now they were becoming as apart from her as her family. She no more belonged here than she had ever belonged anywhere. As if he could hear her thoughts, Tommy suddenly crawled from his place next to her to the back seat. In a moment he and Peggy were necking as though Becky were invisible. Becky glanced at them in the rear view mirror and smiled wryly to herself. There were, after all, only two things men cared about – money and sex. For Tommy, the money part wasn't working so he doubled up on the sex end of it.

Cold air rushed through the open windows and blew her long brown hair around her face, whipping each strand into a tiny lash to sting her face and open the hidden doors of her mind where memories of her stepfather lived. The terror and horror lay only a few layers deep behind the doors, the sleepless hours wondering whether he would come, when he would come, whether she would be able to keep from screaming when he did. Only when she heard him snoring in the next room could she sleep. She could still feel his coarse skin on hers. She could still smell his breath coming hard and fast over her face and into her nostrils.

She pulled off the state highway and onto the long driveway to the house. Ancient pines rose tall and straight into the night sky, filling her head with their overpowering fragrances and dwarfing her ugly memories. The house lay ahead, silhouetted against the sunless sky. Becky was glad she had brought company.

"Wow," Peggy breathed when Becky opened the front door." I would die for this!" It impressed, Becky had to admit. The wide pine floor boards were partially covered by hand-loomed rugs from Arizona. The mantel of the huge stone fireplace supported ivory carvings from the Arctic. Hand-crafted copper chandeliers hung from the twelve foot ceilings. The tall windows were framed by hand-loomed three-toned golden drapes as heavy as rugs. The open staircase led to a wooden bridge which spanned the living room, connecting the bedrooms on the second floor to her studio and Joe's. For a moment she saw it all through Peggy's eyes.

"Come on," she yelled and ran into the kitchen. The room, even at dusk, glistened from the white Formica counter tops and the white appliances. Only a black kerosene stove which provided them with cooking facilities and a modicum of heat during power outages jarred the gleam. Large baskets of overflowing green plants hung from between the twin skylights that allowed views of the blue sky or clouds or wonderful combinations of both during the day and of the stars and moon on cloudless nights.

In the living room she retrieved a long plastic box from under the stereo and fished through it for some head-banging music. She inserted Van Halen's OU812 and cranked up the volume so that the music almost shattered her ear drums and stopped her brain from rerunning the old memories that had started on the way home. Tommy returned from the kitchen with cans of beer for all of them, dropped two of them on the coffee table for Peggy and Becky and then sprawled on the white canvas chaise near the front sliders, gulping his beer, and smoking a long cigarette, imagining himself on top of Becky. She could tell exactly what he was thinking from the leer on his face. He watched her move around the room, while he destroyed his cigarette in an already-full ashtray and lit another one, his eyes glued to her body.

Peggy didn't wait for an invitation to explore the house. She ran upstairs, flipping on light switches as she careened from one room to the next, shrieking ecstatically as she progressed.

Becky leaned back into the softness of the pale green leather couch and closed her eyes to let the music in. The pounding heavy metal cleared her head and finally drew her up from the couch to convulse to the hard rhythms. Her body absorbed the beat until it became part of her and she could be just another instrument that played the music. But then Tommy was there, interrupting her privacy, pulling her body up against his. She closed her eyes as they moved together for a moment. He swung her out away from him, then back, holding her close for just an instant, then away again, finally letting go of her hand so she could dance alone again. She knew he was watching but she didn't care. She came alive when she danced. Her good, strong body moved at her command. She controlled it. It belonged to her and no other person. She pushed Tommy away when he tried to touch her a second time.

Without warning, Peggy screeched down the staircase. "This is the greatest place I ever saw!" she declared. "Let me work for you, Beck. Come on."

Becky looked at her watch. It was 7:00. "Joe's coming soon," she whispered conspiratorially. "You've got to get out before he gets here. He'll kill all of us."

"You don't expect us to walk back to town, do you?" Peggy complained. "Besides, we need to talk about my job."

"Tomorrow, Peg," Becky said. "Come on. I'll take you back to town."

She sent Peggy upstairs to turn off the lights while she turned off some of the downstairs lights.

Tommy grabbed at her as she moved from room to room but she eluded him easily. His reaction time had been halved by beer and whatever else he had been drinking.

It was just 7:15 when she dropped Peggy and Tommy off at the cafe. It was snowing lightly and that meant that Joe would probably be delayed. There was time if she didn't stay too long. She turned the Jeep north for a short distance and then off the highway onto the dirt road that led to the Tree. It was as white as the half-full moon. It seemed almost human, perhaps a young boy with arms outstretched towards the stars. She stumbled through the rough grass, tripping a couple of times, falling once but not hurting herself. She stood at the edge of the bluff with the moon, almost cloud-hidden now, behind her and searched the Tree once more for its secrets.

The slender root sustained it. It had stood alone, unbraced and unguarded, with the least sustenance from and connection to its nurturer, the earth, and yet it had survived for hundreds of years. With her fists she wiped away the tears that rolled unbidden from her eyes. Perhaps she was beginning to understand.

Perhaps she should cry more often. She held her watch up to the pale moonlight. It was 7:45. She ran to the Jeep and jammed it into low gear, roared down the dirt road without regard for how she was jarred back and forth. Joe would be very angry if she weren't there when he got home.

By the time she pulled into their driveway it was 8:30. Joe was obviously home. The lights she had left burning were off.

Only the lights in his studio were on. He had to be working up there, waiting for her to come home. He would never believe she had been out to the Witch Tree at this time of the night.

His car must be in the garage. Becky shuddered. There would be a terrible fight about where she'd been and the condition of the house. There would be tears about her empty easel, about his disappointment with her. There would be the anger for wasting her time and not disciplining herself the way an artist must, and then the ultimate forgiveness she would grant him for his loss of self-control.

She wheeled the Jeep in front of the house and ran inside. "Joe!" she called, but no one answered. She turned on the living room lights and ran through the room, then quickly up the stairs and across the bridge to his studio where the only lights burned.

She paused for a moment to catch her breath and regain control of herself. Then she pushed the door open gently so as not to startle him.

"Joe," she called softly into the enormous room. There was no answer.

The studio was full of Joe's work, his paintings and sketches and paints and brushes and empty canvases awaiting his ideas. She found the studio extraordinarily depressing and rarely went in except to clean it.

In the middle of the room stood an easel with a canvas far smaller than the ones on which Joe usually worked. Becky had never seen it before. Perhaps Joe had finally started working on what was important to him instead of his huge historical monstrosities. Becky pulled it around carefully into the best light.

A blue sky, an exceptional blue sky, a bluff above the lake growing tall, scraggly, rough grasses, and the outline of a small tree hanging out above the lake, a pale, almost white tree, twisted through the years into unimagined shapes and shadows but firmly anchored to the earth, her Tree, her magic, her life – all this leaping from the canvas before her, Joe finally taking it all and making it a part of his being and body.

With a few simple strokes of his brushes he had grasped the essence of the tree and explained its existence. He had clearly reached a new level of consciousness with his work but it was her consciousness that he had invaded, the place where she resided alone and safe from the world. Her heart pounded in her chest like a separate being demanding exit from its prison. She jammed her nails into the flesh of her hands to see if she were still there.

The studio was completely silent. Even the lake seemed silent, its usual lapping sounds against the rocks of the shore muffled by the fine, misting white snow.

She left the painting on the easel and tiptoed out of the room softly, so quietly that not one part of the room would be disturbed, shut the door, hurried across the bridge, down the stairs, across the living room and into the kitchen. She turned on a single light over the gleaming white stove that sat so pristinely, so properly between the two windows that looked out on the driveway. There was no sound of a car. Only the Jeep sat silent and waiting. There was no sound at all. She stared at the stove for a moment, considering its nature. After a moment she finally knew what it was she had to do to save herself.

She moved silently across the kitchen and into the hall that led to the laundry room. A small mountain of dirty clothes awaited her attention. She found two sheets which she could twist into a long rope. She tied the sheets together and then carefully pulled them and turned them until they resembled a rope. She felt as though she had done all of it before, that somehow she was finally performing something she had engineered in her mind a thousand times.

In the garage she found two cans of the kerosene they used for the auxiliary stove in the kitchen. She took them and a bucket back to the laundry room. She poured the kerosene into the bucket and then dipped the sheet rope into the liquid again and again until it was thoroughly soaked. The smell of the fumes made her feel sick for just a moment and then the feeling passed, pushed out of her mind by the impetus of the plan she was executing. She carried the sheet-rope into the kitchen and laid it on the counter next to the stove.

She knew there were emergency candles in the big miscellaneous drawer below where she put everything that didn't belong somewhere else. Under three screwdrivers and a hammer she found a fat white candle and matches. Quietly, carefully, she pushed open the window over the counter next to the stove and dropped them outside.

She pushed the rope between the gas stove and the counter until it was firmly anchored, then fed it through the window, letting it fall the three feet to the dirt below, Then she pushed the window back down just enough to hold the rope in place.

Becky slowly and deliberately opened the four burner jets on the stove and the jet on the oven. The house was still silent. She stayed just long enough to smell gas and then silently, quickly crossed the room, the front hall, opened the front door and went outside. She found the end of the rope and pulled it out across the dirt between the two shrubs below the kitchen window. She lit the candle and twisted it into the soft dirt next to the end of the rope. Then she fed the rope into the candle until it caught fire, dropped it and ran to the Jeep.

She had reached the main highway when the stove gas exploded, lighting the night sky in a spectacular burst of flames. Becky turned the Jeep north towards Canada, north, away from the Witch Tree. Her face burned with the flames of the fire behind her and the fire in her mind that consumed the pale limbs of her prison.

— *Jane Stinson*

The Jewelrymaker

Dear Fithian, when we met in the vineyard,
under a September canopy of hardwoods,

you manned a booth selling photographs
shrunk and decoupaged to mylar.

While curious ladies swarmed,
a riotous orange maple leaf

fastened to velvet fixed my eyes,
I drew my fingers over the smooth surface.
We bartered pin for poem,
safely giving ourselves away.

Your elegant hand on a thin envelope
speaks of connections spoken and unspoken,

conversation to pick up,
the one when I said, "I paint to be color."

Thought, but did not say, "One day I will
roll naked across white canvas,

hairs and pores picking up pigments,
like a lost language. Oil paint

on my breath will beg a smeary kiss
skidding off onto pliant cheeks."

These are things I write to you
but you are not my lover

so they stay here, passing my husband's eyes,
who bids me to follow any trail,

as long as I return to him.
This is hard. The reigning in to one path.

Choice shaped by familiar skin,
giving enough and not enough.

If I met you with red-gloved hands,
how could we resist?

Today I am dangerous
and can smash a world to bits.

— Cheryl Della Pelle

To Matt and Scott

Who are they
the two young men
standing now on the
ceremonial block?
What did they wish to say
to friends assembled
on their behalf?
Out in the world
they are bashed, mocked,
and yet revered for their talents,
artists, dancers, actors.
Creativity runs hard and fast
in their blood.

Too many lights have gone out
too many dead.
And yet these two
hold hands and kiss
ready to take a vow
to love each other, always.
Hold fast family, friends,
ride their wild waves
and beat the drums,
They're out, the closet
is flooded with light and love.

— *Peg Sweeney*

The Primordial Consciousness of Dark Red Lovers

The cool down,
a shaggy blue-grey sky
shakes itself out,
all around hums,
muses out loud
about sun-browned skin
that still smells as warm as
the dark red longing,
for a remembered lover
or one who could be,
who knows there is no time
for lowered lids,
stares the only moment
straight in the face
before the chill sets in,
while the light is still good.

Screaming frenzied heads,
a rush of dahlias knows nothing
of restraint or little passions,
all around hums,
a deep earth rumble
and I come to you with a human face,
born and dying,
satisfied for now to watch wild turkeys
fatten up on buckwheat grass,
but see you down low
with a look that says everything
about desire and I tire of words,
want only my dark red longing
cured by a wild lover, pungent
as snapped stems, flesh, flushed
before the chill sets in,
while the light is still good.

— *Cheryl Della Pelle*

Learning to Speak

A word,
itself the whole sentence,
but a verb only
action pure action;
no subject no object,
never modified;
a verb unchanging,
no past or future,
no over-and-gone,
no not-yet –
never that!

Forever.

We did not then know what
Forever
meant –
means.

For the ever
that is this
     day
     year
     moment –
For the ever
that is not
     all of them
     together.

All of them
one,
one only –
So no
     of-them.

The Forever
that is this one
    held
    embraced
    kissed –
that is this
    one mouth
    one breath
    one flesh –
that is not
    an everyone,
    anyone.

The Forever
that is
    Me.
    Me only.
    Both of Me.
    So: Us
always,
all these ways to be.

— *Robley Whitson*

Aurelia Field at The Longhorn Cafe

I am Aurelia Field
and when I drink I drink
Irish Whiskey, long and lean,
and when the music stops,
a hand slides down
with a green paper in it,
I recognize a ticket, a monetary prize
for a momentary song,
but not this time,
this time I push the buttons,
backlit neon orange
and know this time the song will last
beyond the last call,
I hear it still, hear it?

Back home the night tosses me gently
on the waves of clean sheets.
In my sleep I push away auburn hair
reeking with smoke. Tomorrow I will
wash it and remember

stories told of slave ships to Connecticut
and ghosts who roam Litchfield mansions,
remember crooked rails
and a straight ahead need to connect
life to life
while someone invisible sits alone,
having forgotten how to speak,
how to know when to say
"I am here."

— *Cheryl Della Pelle*

Part III
Misterioso

When the Ravens Assemble

Black feathers pour out of the sky,
swoop down from crags in rock-face
to take a big, black bird-shape.

Raven speaks in a commanding voice
gathers his tribe for a conference
and tells of how the blue sky loves itself.

No matter who is watching, a large female
shakes out her loose feathers,
and a nearby woman tidies up her house that
holds her life.

Two elders stride through tall grass,
bow black heads together in confidence,
speak about the location of a fresh deer
carcass.

When I walk out later, green grass holds
shook feathers as thin black banners
that remind me to pay attention to Raven,

To take a raucous message back into myself
where many worlds whirl in the great dance,
where we are called to learn how to fly,

and to then get on with it, fly, fly, fly.

— *Cheryl Della Pelle*

People Pictures

Painting in the dark
everything night black
     the black mix of all pigments,
     the black absence of color.
When I finish the last
there will be a retrospective,
the body of my life work:
On wall after wall
     black on black on black.
Everyone will be there
nibbling at exotic tastes,
sipping bubbled wine
from crystal glasses,
and talking ear ache talking
in trailed off artspeak sentences
without verbs or periods.

I will watch from somewhere
as they recognize their portraits
on the featureless canvas squares.
The last of the proto-realists,
I paint pictures of people
     only of people,
so I paint in the dark.

— *Robley Whitson*

Light Source

The light changed
becoming crystalized.
Water reached the shore
in great finger holds.
Blueberry bushes ran
along the road's edge
climbing up into long
rocky fields.
Time was lost
in clothes blowing on a line.
Old farm houses flying flags.
White porches decked
with red geraniums.

Indeed, what can
I tell you
of light and air
wind, water and sky?
Time turned inside out
and upside down.
Watches, clocks, faceless.
Children running free
on beaches washed
by endless time.
Time so finally lost
it is found.

— Peg Sweeney

Open One Eye

I intend to open an eye –
either one first,
only later the other.
Never both together at once;
just one at a time.

Otherwise dimensions happen,
lines of sight
leading off from me
to a vanishing point.

If I look with both eyes
it will be there to see,
then the next thing
will be to go to it,
and into it.

And I know
there will be no looking back:
to where my eyes were closed,
and I could dream
whatever I wanted,
and everything slipped around
vanishing points
at the last moment,
and I could dream on
and keep looking back,
dream and look.

— Robley Whitson

Sleep Flying

My hair is black as ravens feathers
and my name is Ellsworth.
I walk wherever I go
unless I choose to fly.
It is faster
and how it feels, how it is,
oh, this is not able to be said.

You tumble over yourself
as the stream tumbles over rocks.
Tonight, after rising onto two feet,
you will jump-fly, now.
Run fast, jump and use your arms
like they were wings. See.
You are rising, moving up.
Very good.

As you come down, the ground
will meet you gently,
as if you are a fallen leaf.
Remember this
and use it wisely.
You are not special,
you merely know better, clearer,
that you are not completely earthbound.

— *Cheryl Della Pelle*

Manitoba Night Prairie

The crescent-shaped moon
hangs golden in the
vast prairie sky
its promise of fullness
like a young girl
etched in a circle of light.

Across the horizon line
millions of stars stretch
becoming star soldiers
young men, dead, before their time,
banished forever to the sky
still vainly seeking
the crescent moon's promise.

Ribbons of light blue and scarlet
slowly fill the eastern sky.
Dawn erases the star soldiers
leaving only Venus
shining hopefully on.

Manitoba prairie
stretching across day and night,
moon touching earth
stars burning ever on.
Time rising on the back light
         of the moon.

— *Peg Sweeney*

Part IV
Grave

The Awakening

There was a moment, once, when all things changed; the sun became the moon, day night, truth a lie, the future the dark lost present. Allatonce jumbling, tumbling, stumbling, juggling, trembling, a screaming timelesseternity, a neverending second, reality nightmare, clarity blindness — a moment suspended and extended, a moment multiplied and divided, squared and reduced to No Thing. What I knew became ignorance, what had been whole was shattered. Was it the dream we all fear yet dream, was it a nightmare, an illusion — could time wind and unwind like a watch. Is time outside the frame that defines the infinite.... destiny discovered me.... was it cause or effect....

The grass was June green, past the innocence of spring, a filling out green was growing that would ripen dark in August. The sky was childhood blue and yet it seemed like a wide Southwest sky, expansive beyond thought. The earth rolled its hills and Mennonite and Amish farms throughout the land of Pennsylvania.

It was early June, 1968. That spring Knoxville had seen gas cans filled with rage in the back of pick-up trucks, outfitted with loaded rifles to fire the bullets of insanity after Martin Luther King was shot down in Memphis. Two months later Robert Kennedy was felled in a hotel in California in that nightmare way America has of silencing the voices of the courageous. That spring I was finished with the South, finished with its bigotry, its white and colored rest rooms, white and colored water fountains, white and colored, colored became Black and Black became Afro-American but only the names changed, the bridge wasn't really crossed, nor the wounds healed. There was progress in the Panthers, progress but not quick enough, not deep enough. That spring I was finished with the South.

America was coming apart. I had just passed my oral exams and my thesis had been accepted. I would receive my M.A. in English by mail. I wanted out of the South. I had been there from 1962-1968, the sixties in the South. They had been hard years for a rebellious, white, free-thinking Yankee woman. I was twenty-two years old and I was going home, back to Connecticut to figure out the next step. I was tired of the South, and just as tired of Academia with its analysis of every word written. There was a senselessness everywhere; assassination, prejudice, violence, red-faced, red-necked hatred suffocated me. I was ready for a change.

My mother flew down to Knoxville to help me pack and make the drive north. She was sixty-two years old. Hers was not a happy marriage. She had been a nurse when she met my father. She helped put him through medical school at the University of Tennessee. She had five pregnancies; two children survived, my brother and me. There had been one miscarriage, one child stillborn and one infant crib death. My father became a successful radiologist and my mother became the doctor's wife. When I was twelve or thirteen she began to paint. She loved it. It was hers alone but he always signed her paintings, printing her name on the canvas. She told me once that she had written poetry, quite a bit of it, but that my father found it and burned it all years ago. My mother — who had been orphaned at the age of six with her brother, their parents having died within one year of each other, her mother of T.B. and her father in a train wreck — was Catholic. My father was a non-practicing agnostic Jew of immigrant parents. His father died when he was eleven years old and left his mother with five children to raise, and run an East Boston grocery store.

I came to learn, but not to understand, that my father forbade my mother to practice her religion. His mother had thrown my mother out of her house because she was Catholic. I guess one forbids what is threatening.

When I was a young girl, my mother and I would drive out of town, away from New Haven and its environs. She would search for a Catholic church, in whatever city or town we found ourselves. My experience of her religion, besides knowing she kept a crucifix hidden in her scarf and glove drawer, was the empty churches we visited with lighted candles and statues and holy water and the smell of devotion. Sometimes I would see someone in the church, kneeling, fingering rosary beads and saying prayers.

I would watch my mother light candles, kneel before the statue of the Virgin Mother, take out her hidden rosary beads and pray. I wondered who and what she prayed for, this devoted woman, denied and forbidden her religion. I had once witnessed my father, in a rage rip apart her amethyst rosary and throw the beads across the room at her.

The church was a haven where I was able to see the relief on my mother's face. So often, it seemed to me, she lived in fear of his arm being raised against her, or my brother. When my father would threaten to hit my brother, my mother would place herself between them, taking the blow. On the days that we'd find refuge in a church, I could see her relax, exhale, as though she'd been holding her breath between these visits. It seemed to me that my father was as jealous of her devotion to her religion as he might have been had she been with a lover.

This June trip to Knoxville was an unusual one for my mother. Although she traveled all over the world with my father, she rarely traveled alone. This was a week of freedom for her. When she arrived I was studying for my orals and it was a tense time. She expressed her hope to me that perhaps she might finally leave my father and live with me, temporarily, until she knew what she was going to do. I was caught in the worlds of Milton, Shakespeare, Kennedy, King, and my mother's burgeoning hopes of emancipation.

The oral exams passed, thesis accepted, bags packed, rented furniture returned, we drove out of Knoxville heading north. We spent the first night of the trip in a motel. Early the following morning we breakfasted on pancakes, coffee, and laughter, and headed home. The sky was clear and I quoted Byron, Yeats, Shakespeare, and Ernest Dowson.

They are not long, the weeping and the laughter,
Love and desire and hate,
I think they have no portion in us after
We pass the gate.
They are not long the days of wine and roses,

Out of a misty dream our paths emerge
Then close within a dream.

ALLATONCE the car, a black 1962 Mercedes, a heavy car, caught its tires in the gravel, and to avoid the median, I swerved too far to the right and veered off the highway and was catapulted over the edge, turning over and over and over, my mother's body covering mine as we tumbled over and over and over, the top becoming the bottom and the bottom falling out of everything. We landed at the bottom of a ravine. When I came to, I had no idea how long I had been unconscious – seconds, minutes or hours. Time had been fractured and would never tick or pulse or beat the same way again. I checked my mother. I looked into her eyes and felt her pulse and knew that she was dead. I saw her fingers crushed, what did broken bones matter when her breath was gone. I cried for what happened so quickly. I closed her eyes, that stared outward to a heavenly world I had escaped. "I killed her," I screamed over and over to the world. I screamed to the nothingness that surrounded me, to the void that engulfed me. "I killed her," echoed through this space of suspended life. I tried the door but couldn't get out. There was shattered glass everywhere. Everything was shattered. I tried to believe that I was asleep, that this was a nightmare, that I had learned my lesson, but no — I checked her again, seeing now her broken neck. I was there alone with her for nearly an hour, trapped with guilt and tears and fears as my only company. Finally, a gentle greyhaired black man called for help as I screamed, "I killed her" over and over.

"No, little lady, never think that. It was an accident, a terrible accident...." The ambulance came, I screamed for the men to take my mother first. They put us both on stretchers and rolled us into the back of the ambulance, my mother and me, side by side, dead and alive; we drove to a hospital, drove side by side to the end that spring.

Now I knew the unknowable place between life and death and nothing was ever the same again.

— *Davyne Verstandig*

The Deep of Tears

Unhidden faces seen
through streaks of rain,
eyes and mouths
in wet running lines
on glass panes –
    eyeing insides of drops
    escaped from open sky,
    mouthing overheard words
    in storms of sounds
    that fly overhead
    surrounding infinite bones
    curved and stretched out
    articulated into dreams –
who distort to stir
from sleeps of rain,
who ever peer in on us
through our smeary windows.

—*Robley Whitson*

Warrior Women

Warrior Women write
of feelings deep, wild,
pushing up, out,
feelings stuffed, crushed
held in by guilt
or lessons well learned.

Warrior Women write
of abuse
by fathers, uncles, grandfathers,
brothers, friends
who pretended to love
but felt, caressed, penetrated
young girls, innocent in their age,
warned not to tell.

Warrior Women write
crying out to be heard
pointing the finger,
challenging mothers who
froze in submission
to beatings and threats
or said they didn't know.

Warrior Women write
holding the pen
writing on and on.
The healing takes
so very long.

— Peg Sweeney

Shift

Find the rubber handled ignition key that has slipped
    down into a pocket of tear in tweed's satin lining.
Button up coat and turn on headlights.
Push the black bar and skim airwaves for a Motown sound.
Listen to NPR's update on Guantanamo Bay turn into
    New England's incoming blizzard report.
Feel angry for political caging.
Be thankful for deep treaded snow tires.
Leave the state pavement for dirt roaded home.
Take dirt road and surrender steering to frozen, casted rut.
Follow rut into steep bank.
See road ahead sideways.
Flip car over onto roof.
Hear metal scratch and safety glass split.
See road up side down.
Scream anything obscene.
Calm down.
Scream again.
Turn engine off.
Locate shattered window by cold air rush.
Use seat cushions above to pull your body out.
Get on foot and stumble.
Crawl.
Grasp for full breath but pant.
Unlock your house door.
Have the frozen key stick to your bloody fingers.
Make sure that you don't need an ambulance.
Dial telephone for help.
Find flashlight walk back to wreck.
Make icicle tears.

— *Kellie Campbell*

Not Yet

Intimately
intimidated
by a breathing
not all my own –
    as slight as a sigh
    flowing through the dreams
    of dry leaves
    beneath fallen trees –
the sign of things
said all wrong
so long ago,
dead but ungrieved –
not yet gone off
far enough.

— *Robley Whitson*

Touch

White coated doctor
Mouths verdict of
Mastectomy, or lumpectomy
With matter of fact words,
Never shedding tears
Or reaching out hands
To reassure the woman
Who listens.

He forgets he once was
Comforted and nurtured
At a woman's breast
Given life, while now
Life may be lost.

White coated Doctor
Sitting safely behind his desk
Unable, afraid, to reach out
Forgetting healing, life,
    begins
        with
            touch.

— *Peg Sweeney*

The Moon Guided Me Home Tonight

Beneath close cropped finger nails, a garden
of coffee ground black soil. Castings of purple
liatris and stark white cosmos – bursting in day.
Afternoon under alpine light, shadows split
weeping pines, also me into two. Eight hours I nurse
flower borders. Twenty-four I am lonely.

Speeding to tempt her I meditate until calm. Black
bra coddles breasts yearing for light like dandelions
for spring. I want more than chamomile in a porcelain
cup. More than my body can promise alone.

— Kellie Campbell

Part V
Teneroso

SOUL MATES
A Play in One Act

Scene 1. *A dining room table. Four place mats. An ashtray. A cup and saucer. A glass of milk and a box of cookies. Mother and Son are seated opposite. She is in her 70s, frail and pale, but with the strength of a survivor. Her hand shakes as, alternately, she drinks tea and smokes a cigarette. He is in his 30s, uncomfortable in the role of comforter.*

SON: *(to audience)* When my father died I took the cinerary urn containing his ashes from the hall closet and put it in the glove compartment of the family car, a 1974 gold-colored Plymouth Valiant with a black vinyl roof. I did this without my mother's knowledge. My father had loved his car almost as much as his other great love, the New York Mets. I knew he would be happier in the car, where we could listen to a game once in a while, instead of being stuffed away in the back of a closet with all those memories – so close to... her. *(Pause)* On the drive home from the funeral parlor she – my mother, that is – sat with the urn on her lap. At one point I turned to look at her and she was fondling the urn with her fingers and crying. When we got home she put the urn back in the box it came in and shoved it to the back of the closet. *(Turning to MOTHER)* You're not going to keep his ashes in the closet are you?

MOTHER: *(Exhaling smoke)* That's where I want them. Why aren't you drinking your milk?

SON: That's no place for them. Why don't you let me put them somewhere else?

MOTHER: No.

SON: But why not?

MOTHER: Because I don't want you to. Isn't that enough reason? I want them in the closet. *(She begins to weep.)* Why are you so stubborn?

SON: That's no place for them.

MOTHER: *(Wailing)* Leave me alone. It's where I want them.

(MOTHER and SON fall silent. He looks at her stonily as she stares into space with tears in her eyes. Then, after a moment...) It would have been sixty years in September. Sixty years...

SON: He had a good life.

MOTHER: I only wish he could have lived to see all of you together one last time. That was what he wanted – more than anything.

SON: Don't start that again...please! You know there's no way Ellen and I are getting back together.

MOTHER: How he wanted that.

SON: *(to audience)* She means it's what she wanted. All he wanted was to go on a cruise. In the end it was her constant nagging that killed him.

FATHER: *(Entering the room. He is in his 80s, small, grandfatherly.)* Janet, have you got a little something for lunch?

MOTHER: Lunch? You just ate breakfast.

FATHER: That was four hours ago.

MOTHER: I think if I let you, you'd eat all day.

FATHER: A little something for lunch, Janet. That's all I want.

MOTHER: You don't need any lunch.

FATHER: *(Forgetting about lunch.)* You know, Janet, I've been thinking, it might be nice to go on a cruise – like the ones they advertise in the paper – to Bermuda.

MOTHER: *(Snickering)* Bermuda? You want me to go on a cruise to Bermuda...with you? You can't even remember to take your pills. How do you expect to go on a cruise?

FATHER: No, I mean it, Janet. Let's go on a cruise.

MOTHER: You and your ideas. I'm no going on any cruise with you. That's all I need is for something to happen...

FATHER: So what could happen? I could die? I could die on a boat just as easily as I could die in my own house.

MOTHER: *(Looking at him with disgust.)* You know, Lou, you make me sick.

SON: I don't understand. Why are you talking to him like that? A cruise doesn't sound like a bad idea.

MOTHER: I told you I'm not going on any cruise with him. You know, you're stupid. You're both stupid.

FATHER: *(Waving his hand at her in disgust)* I don't know how I've lived with you all these years, Janet. Don't go. Don't go. I don't give a God-damn. I'll go by myself. Meanwhile, I'm going in to watch the ball game. *(Father exits. Mother continues to drink tea and puff on her cigarette.)*

SON: *(to audience)* He died the next day. I was at a friend's house when my aunt called. "You better go to your mother," she said. "Your father's dead." I'm sure he died on purpose. He was determined to take that trip one way or another. Well, he did. He fooled her after all. It was okay with me. We had made our peace, he and I.

MOTHER: Oh God, what am I going to do?

SON: You can come live with me.

MOTHER: With you?

SON: Yes, with me.

MOTHER: You've got some case. You want me to come live with you, the way you live?

SON: And how do I live?

MOTHER: If you have to ask, don't expect me to tell you.

SON: Oh, I see. So you don't want to live with me. Then what do you want? You can't just sit in this house and vegetate. You can't sit and watch television all day.

MOTHER: I won't just sit and watch television. I have plenty to do.

SON: Like what?

MOTHER: I've got cleaning.

SON: Yeah?

MOTHER: I've got bills to pay.

SON: Yeah?

MOTHER: I've got plenty to do. Don't worry about me.

Scene 2. *The garage. The cinerary urn is on the roof of the car. The son is cleaning the windshield with a rag. The sound of a ball game can be heard coming from inside the car.*

SON: You know, Dad, if she finds out about this, we're both dead. *(Suddenly, there is a lot of excitement on the radio.)* Wait a minute. Listen. All right. Kingman hit a homer! Go Mets! You know, Dad, you should have waited out the season. The Mets might just make it to the pennant. *(He starts whistling "Take Me Out to the Ball Game".)* How did you whistle the way you did, Dad? You couldn't sing, you couldn't play a musical instrument. How did you do it? *(He whistles some more, then falls flat.)* You know, Dad, I have to tell you this car is pretty ugly. I know, you don't have to remind me, I picked it out. But that's because it was the only one they had with a V-8 engine. I knew how you loved V-8s. Remember the Packard – the '53 Packard? That was a straight 8. Remember that? Those days are gone forever. You know Dad, I never did tell you this, but that time you and Mom went to California and left me home alone – the time I nearly burnt the house down cooking a TV dinner – I took the Packard out for a little spin. The car was so wide I smacked into the door frame trying to back out of the garage. You never noticed, though. God, was I scared. I was so scared I was shaking. The only other time I shook that bad was once when I slept with a blind woman. Can you believe that? I don't know why I was so scared then, but I couldn't stop shaking. She thought I was cold. I don't know, it just didn't seem right, sleeping with her. There was something so exciting about it though. *(Continues cleaning, silently)* I'm always judging myself. I always do that. I judge everything. I can't let things be, on their own terms. You – you were never very judgmental. You just let things happen. You never really thought about anything, did you? I'll bet you never even stopped to think why you lived with Mom for so many years. She never had a decent word to say to you. She cheated on you. I bet you didn't know that. She did. I remember, I was nine years old and it was summer vacation; mom and I were staying at a bungalow in the country. You worked during the week and came up on weekends. Well, one weekday night I was in bed. I was supposed to be sleeping when Mom came home with a strange man. I could hear them kissing in the living room. I knew something wasn't right, but I was too scared to get up. Can you believe it? Mom! Having an affair! Ha. What about you? Did you ever have an affair? I'll bet you did. But then, I never really knew anything about you, did I? To me, you were always a grandpa – first sixty, then seventy, then eighty. God it was awful. Did you know that when I was little I always thought you were going to die because you were older than all the other kids' dads? Remember when you had that heart condition? One night I was lying in bed with the light on and I started listening to the beating of my own heart. As I listened, the sound got louder and louder; pretty soon it sounded as if it was going to explode. I got so scared that I jumped out of bed and ran into the bathroom and threw up.... So what do you think, Dad? What's going to be with Mom? She just sits there in front of the TV all day. She doesn't get dressed. She doesn't do anything. Not that she did much before you died. At least then she had your meals to make, and she could yell at you a few times a day. But now...now she doesn't do anything. She won't even touch the piano. Every time I mention it she gets weepy. She says, "Oh, I remember how your father used to sit on the couch and whistle while I played." That's what she says now. What about all those years she screamed at you? "Why can't you make more money? Why can't you be a better father? What kind of a husband are you?" How did you stand it? Now she talks about how wonderful it was. Can you believe it?

Scene 3. *MOTHER and SON are sitting on easy chairs on opposite sides of the stage. Next to each chair is an end table with a lamp and a telephone. MOTHER is holding the receiver to her ear. The other phone is ringing. SON answers it.*

SON: Hello.

MOTHER: Harry?

SON: Mom. Hi. How are you doing?

MOTHER: Harry, your father's gone.

SON: What are you talking about?

MOTHER: Your father's gone. His ashes are gone from the closet. I don't know who would do such a sick thing, but someone has taken him.

SON: Unnh...Mom...I...unnh...they...unnh..his ashes aren't gone. I have them.

MOTHER: *(After a moment of silence.)* You...have...them?

SON: Yes, I have them. They're...he's...I...it's in the car.

MOTHER: In the car? What are they doing in the car?

SON: They've been there since Dad died.

MOTHER: Since he died? That was two years ago. Your father has been in the car for two years?

SON: Well, not exactly. I mean it's not really Dad who's in the car. After all...it's only his ashes.

MOTHER: What do you mean only his ashes? What are they doing there?

SON: I...he...you...I just didn't think they belonged in the closet.

MOTHER: I want them in the house, do you hear me. I want them in the house, now!

SON: Now?

MOTHER: Now!

SON: But mom, I can't come over there now.

MOTHER: *(Crying.)* Then when can you come?

SON: Friday. Maybe I can come on Friday.

MOTHER: Not 'til Friday? All right, then come for dinner on Friday. I want those ashes in the house.

SON: All right. All right. I'll bring them in.

MOTHER: Don't forget. I'll see you Friday. Good-bye.

SON: Good-bye.

Scene 4. *The garage. Same as before. SON is cleaning the car. A Mets game is playing on the car radio. Dave Kingman is at bat.*

SON: Come on Kingman. You can do it. *(Kingman strikes out.)* Kingman, you slob. Where did you learn to play baseball? *(Looks up at the urn.)* He's never there when you need him, you know. *(He reaches for the urn, takes it, and retrieving a box from inside the car, places the urn in it.)* Well Dad, this is it: our last game together. I'm really sorry. I'm going to miss you. You know, this is the closest we've ever been, these past two years. You've helped me to understand a lot of things. I know you lover her, but I still think you should have left her a long time ago. I think both of you would have been better off. You taught me something, though. I made my decision before it was too late. You know how I knew when it was time for me to go? Remember how you used to wave your hand at Mom when you were disgusted at something, (demonstrates) like this? Well, I started doing the same thing. I could hear you telling me, "Don't be weak like I was." Well, I guess this is it. I'm real sorry to see you go back into the closet; but who knows... maybe later there'll be a chance to get you out of there. Until then, spend some time with those memories for a while. You know, the last time I went through that closet, I actually found your old gas mask...I guess it was from World War I. And a book of ration stamps from the '40s. You'll be in good company. So long. (He closes the box.)

Scene 5. *Same as scene 1, except MOTHER and SON meet at the front door. He is carrying the box.*

MOTHER: Where is it? *(He hands her the box. She takes it and puts it on a shelf in an open closet near the entrance. They both go to the dining room table, which is set as before, except this time there are dinner plates on the table. He sits first. She goes offstage and returns carrying a platter of spaghetti. She serves him. She puts the platter down and goes offstage again and returns with a container of milk. She pours him a glass and sits down.)*

SON: Well, I guess I'll sell the car.

MOTHER: So sell the car. Why aren't you eating? Drink your milk.

SON: I'm eating, I'm eating. And I don't want milk. *(He pushes the glass away. They sit silently for a few moments. She lights a cigarette. She is obviously annoyed. For a while she stares at him angrily while he eats.)*

MOTHER: You know, you're stupid. You're really stupid.

— *Marc Erdrich*

The Button Box

A rusted blue harlequin, his smile faded,
chipped at the corners, emblazons the top
of the tin box.
Before opening a good shake rattles old buttons;
I know them, each one,
and as the lid pops off, the smell of quiet dust
drifts out;
it is the attic above the back stairway
that leads to boxes of books, plastic curtains
that with a breath would disintegrate,
and a forgotten drying rack stands naked.
It is always warm in the attic, and dry,
and I always know who I am there
or who I was.
As I sit at a child's table, on a very small chair
and look out the gable window that overlooks the
garden you used to tend,
I cannot let it go,
someplace, maybe it is here,
but it doesn't have to be the last time I breathe
the air of my childhood, no, I need only remember
to take down your old button box, pry off the lid,
select a favorite button
and hold you in my hand.

— Cheryl Della Pelle

This Is Why

Because I am alive and glad of it,
because the days are gifts although I did not always
know it,
because I might never have been alive,
because I did not die in childhood,
I lived and was glad of it and wanted to live more.

Because I lived, you lived, although I feared for you.
Because you lived, the pain was unimportant,
I paid no attention to it, I failed to heal the pain.

Because I kept on living, others lived,
because they lived I tried to keep on living.

Because life and the days are gifts and I thought you
knew it,
because I had learned to live with difficulty,
because I loved you and trusted you to live ...
I trusted wrong.
I failed to keep you living,
I failed to give you days that were gifts.
The whole world failed to keep you living.

I could not thank the gift of you enough,
I did not pay enough attention to your pain.
Because your courage followed a skewed compass
my heart broke and my tongue froze, watching you.
I did not know, I did not know your road.

Because it is right that I grieve when the leaves
whisper,
grieve when I remember your love
or when I remember my love for you,
grieve when I give your books away,
because it is right that I grieve for my ignorance,

it is right that I grieve for what you knew
and for what you did not know,
for what we knew and did not know.

Because you did not live, you achieved death.
Because I did not die I achieved life,
I did not die, have not died yet.
Because I live with all these gifts of days,
I would divide them with you if I could.

Because I am glad to have the days,
because your pain tempts me to be ashamed of
pleasure
and I refuse that evil,
because I love you and I love my days,
I love the days I had with you.
I love the days that are so full
of living time and space they stretch and creak.
Because I love you and will always love you,
because I thank God that you lived at all,
I offer you my peace,
the only gift I have for you, this year,
this time, this place.

— *Nan Adams*

The Center

Out the window door
lilacs bloom in
wild scented profusion.
Apple blossoms frame
the bright green meadow
setting a velvet stage
for the returning deer.

The old wicker rocker,
newly painted
is placed on the porch.
Its ample seat ready
to welcome friends and animals.
A grandchild calls from
miles away
to tell of radishes we planted in March
now, bright red, and ready to eat.

Lingering, I watch an infant
open tiny hands, wrapping them
around a grandmother's thumb,
eyes and voices meeting,
each holding tightly to new lives
so recently found.

Out the window door lilacs bloom now,
the scent filling the air.
Gathering an armful,
I place them carefully
in the center
            of my room.

— *Peg Sweeney*

For Martha von Rohminger

A sunny porch lifts a hooded face onto
last rays,
I could say I am lonely, empty in a spot,
I could say I miss you.
No one walked through straight pines
as slowly as you and holly hocks fell
into your apron, clipped heads in full bloom,
perfect, no breath;
we sat on cracked wooden steps,
young knees, bony knees,
clear brown legs, freckled weathered legs,
this was us,
your deft hands fashioned dolls from blossoms
and cast a spell over my pony-tailed head.
"Laugh a lot" you said. I have tried not
to waste a single petal of your wisdom,
tortured and true, dug out of garden dirt,
hung on a rope line to dance.

— *Cheryl Della Pelle*

Matins

The cat,
the damn fool cat was the one
I wanted to get shut of –
and it's still around.
Someone else
is gone.
Obviously a mistake.
But you don't make mistakes,
do you, God?
I could have spared the cat.
I could have –
could have done lots of things.
Could have inquired, pressed,
investigated, snooped, done everything
he disliked most.

Instead I listened, waited,
respected, waited, listened,
and, always, respected his space,
his privacy.

Last night was full of bright ideas,
all of them twenty-two days
too late.

— *Nan Adams*

Wall Paper

Monotonous dots walk the walls
on the faded paper
never making up their minds –
    up or down, or
    back or forth, or
    diagonal angle.

They seem to search for something
hidden in the thicket
of wandering rhomboids

it might be a simple square
    dot dot
    dot dot

or the infinities of points that
    roll sun-stars into fire to
    spin off round blue worlds and
    twine helixes into me.

I wait for sleep
and watch them
    creating
watch them
    searching
while I lie here
in plain sight.

— Robley Whitson

Fifty is Nifty
or So They Say

My hands,
reflecting in the mirror
while I touch and probe
groping at the soft nipple
searching for the possible
hidden lump –
with its fear laden message.
Hands, lingering now
touching, caressing the nipples
remembering their hardness
and tenderness
engorged with milk.
Fingers, deftly directing
their flow
into eager, searching mouths.
Rocking back and forth
warm flesh
against my body,
sweet, sour smells,
lullabies softly sung

Now, blasting music
jars my reverie –
as my eyes are drawn
to the window –
outside, adult children play
babbling voices
hurling bodies,
flinging their overgrown selves
in pursuit of a ball.
They're 'hanging out' now
until the laundry's finished
the dinner served
their stomachs full
once again.

— *Peg Sweeney*

Author Index